DEAR LIFE

PREVIOUS AND INTERNATIONAL PRAISE FOR SHANTA ACHARYA

Her poetry has a melody and at the same time a vivid and down-to-earth quality which is really rare today. They are, so to speak, at home with themselves and not at all self-conscious. She often seems to be rescuing real poetry from the kinds of post-modern poeticism which are current today.
John Bayley

Shanta Acharya is concerned with the big, often painful subjects—death and loss, love's shortfalls, poverty and dispossession—but there are moments of humour and satire, and a rich aesthetic delight in the variousness of the world. Acharya's poems are full of the pleasures of the unexpected.
Carol Rumens

It was the Danish physicist, Neils Bohr, who said that a great truth is a truth whose opposite is also a great truth. In poems rooted in the Upanishads, yet connecting through natural imagery with New England transcendentalism, Shanta Acharya summons courage to face such truths. It's hard to write "mystical" poetry these days, yet no other overall vision seems likely to prevent "the vulnerable plot of green," as she says, from being trampled by "frantic minds" not yet clear enough "to defend their humanity" by reconciling contradictions.
Anne Stevenson

Her poetry shows a rare combination of lyricism, intelligence, sagacity and a wicked sense of humour. She is not afraid to tackle large themes, to take on the abstract, metaphysical, spiritual or to use the idiom such themes demand. It is refreshing to find these qualities in such an engaging and individual voice.
Mimi Khalvati

Her clear vision has purged her writing of extraneous sentiment…. She cuts to the heart of things when, in one poem, she advises her readers to "discover in loneliness the continents of yourself."
   Peter Porter

Her acute eye and keen sense of form depict the outer world in vivid detail, invoking the inner world where human experience makes its reality. Here is a poet of much clarity of spirit and a wondrous gift for evoking place.
   Penelope Shuttle

Dreams That Spell The Light is a book…reflecting on the precariousness of life; the wisdom is drawn from a humane understanding of our place in the universe. But there is room for humour and pity and much close observation in these finely honed poems that work across cultures.
   George Szirtes

These poems take on our strange times unflinchingly, and show that they still offer scope for creativity, craft and lyricism, qualities that are now more necessary than ever. A courageous and multifaceted collection.
   Matthew Francis

In language that is accurate, spontaneous, and often witty, Shanta Acharya explores ways in which the modern individual can find a place in the world, having floated free of traditional supports. These are brave and thoughtful poems.
   Carole Satyamurti

There is a stateliness and poise about Shanta Acharya's poetry that is remarkable. Her poetry grapples with life, the vicissitudes of fate, and much beyond. The variety of themes she explores and confronts is formidable – life, art, illusion, death. One observes the integrity of the poet as her true being emerges. This collection has a momentum of its own, the poetry inexorably moving towards an inner core. One puts down the volume with the feeling that one has come face to face with a true established poet.
   Keki Daruwalla

Shanta Acharya has an uncannily poetic way of relating to reality that is deeply Indian without being insular. Hers is a meditative spirit which however seldom abandons its interrogative scepticism that shapes its subtle politics. Her poetry quarrels with power in all its incarnations, divine and human, without ever being loud, and her emotional range is wide, from the pains of a girl growing up in an unkind world to the pleasures of love and the abjectness of abandonment. She realizes that 'knowing is all' and with it too that knowing is agony. Reading these poems together is like entering a house with many windows, each opening on a different landscape.

K. Satchidanandan

Shanta Acharya's poems are inspired by her emotional experiences, for which simple but convincing words, phrases and sound effects have been found. There is nothing artificial in her statements and choice of forms. The complex and profound are equally well expressed in her imagery.

Nissim Ezekiel

The incongruities of life are everywhere in Shanta Acharya's striking and evocative collection of poems. A canal in Camden Town contains fish peering through a golden purdah. Coriander and cinnamon bark evoke love and desire. The poet sprays herself with Nirvana and Eternity. Time rearranges the past, turning home into "a place we've never been before." All we can do, in the teeth of pain, is hang on for *Dear Life*.

Mark Abley

In this paean to life's mysteries, Shanta Acharya takes a stand against everyday caprice and uncertainty: the ravages of war in the Ukraine and Aleppo, exile, the pandemic, and most painfully the death of her brother. Her capacity to wonder at the unexpected and embrace what is irrefutably human and of this world, are sources of hope and renewal in the face of loss. In these finely crafted poems, Acharya's buoyant spiritual reckoning is tempered with wisdom and humour.

Janet Wilson

DEAR LIFE

Shanta Acharya

BOOKS

Los Angeles & London

Book, Jacket and Logo design by Leopard Design Studio.

Cover photo and author portrait by © Dr. Sanjay Acharya.

ISBN 9798218465247 (hc)
ISBN 9798218465292 (sc)
ISBN 9798218465261 (e)

Reviews and Queries should be directed to: poetlee@earthlink.net

Online:
LWL BOOKS at: lanceleeauthor.com
Shanta Acharya at: shanta-acharya.com

ⓁⓌⓁ BOOKS

Los Angeles & London

Not knowing when the Dawn will come
I open every Door.
    Emily Dickinson

In the universe, there are things that are known, and things that are
unknown, and in between, there are doors.
    William Blake

The purpose of poetry is to remind us
how difficult it is to remain just one person,
for our house is open, there are no keys in the doors,
and invisible guests come in and out at will.
    Czesław Miłosz

If you shut the door to all errors, truth will be shut out.
    Rabindranath Tagore

CONTENTS

The Shatkona star ❖ symbolizes the fusion of the masculine and feminine as the source of all creation in Hinduism.

POEMS

BEING ALIVE

Moving through the scanner my body lights
up in a scrum of pain, building images

like slices of a loaf of bread of each organ,
coloured spectrum of stories on a CT-scan,

virtual libraries stacked with contrasting
columns of formularies, offering

drafts of the estates of my exhaustion,
maps of my body's imperfection—

unX-rayed the tempest swelling in my mind,
spasms of hurt bordering on ecstasy,

the way waves of energy dance at the edges
of tiredness, the way autumn colours

seize the day before the grey-white-evergreen
flag of winter hoists herself, before I lose

track of myself, a witch dragging my pain,
splintering down the spine, commanding me

to obey, else rue the day I stopped listening
to my body now branded with the world's

suffering, wiser than the experts who probe
my insides for signs of malaise, failing

to diagnose the cause of my grieving;
the mysterious bleeding a way of speaking,

urging me not to drown in man's inhumanity,
heal myself with love, touchstone of the universe.

SOMETHING TO DO WITH LOVE

Surveying the locked down map of my world,
windows opening to landscapes of uncertainty,
time dances like a god in the changing light.
Dwelling in possibility, I take nothing for granted—
accept life as it comes, not the way I want it.
Something to do with love, a prayer to protect
us from an innocent touch. As the death toll rises,
so do fear and courage. Key workers keep carrying
on, laying bare the injustices of our world.
Knowing there is no going back, we hang on
with the furloughed, believing in blue skies, bird song,
and spring in the dreadful winter of our hearts.
Hope lives like a virus born with a message—
life's a gift, a thing of beauty, cherish it.

LONELINESS

A professional assassin, strikes without warning,
works with exaggerated slowness and precision,
plays a game of cat-and-mouse, leaving me
stunned in a tangle of nerves as it sucks the energy
out of me, flicking my days like images on a screen—
menacing lions ready to drag me into oblivion
when the jungle morphs with flashes of lightning,
and loneliness shows me things I'd never seen—
past and future unfurling in ways unimagined,
my days measured in blister packs of agony.
Lying under the duvet, grief torn, I marvel
at shafts of light that lean in like angels of mercy.
For a brief moment dust appears luminescent,
glowing fireflies dancing in the light.

DRESSING UP IN LOCKDOWN

A pristine summer's day, sparkling like champagne,
perfect for giving my garments an airing.
At home in a bubble of my own, lounging
in pyjama and dressing gown, numbering
my days' illusions, comfort reigns over style.
My wardrobe reprimands me, cries in chorus—
saris complaining the loudest of not being
touched, embraced, admired—their silks, chiffons,
satins, crepes, georgettes, chanderis mothballed
in tissue, chide me for starving myself
in the midst of plenty. Unable to ignore their
pleas, I wear a sari with matching jewellery,
spray myself with Nirvana and Eternity,
with a glass of bubbly watch Downton Abbey.

FORGIVENESS OF BEES

Dancing in riddles, buff-tailed, they buzz and bumble
against the double-glazing—swirling poems
on ecstatic wings, praying without ceasing.
I sit cross-legged, meditating, their swing and jig
the propolis protecting me—the peace of wild things
descends like a mantle woven with blessings.
Day my boiler stopped working, the gasman found
a drift of bees dead inside—warriors, brave
as Abhimanyu who knew how to enter the maze
of life, love and war, the invincible Chakravyuha,
killed for not knowing how to exit the battlefield.
Grief-stricken, unable to warn selfless explorers
that instinct can save or destroy at will, I feel
the forgiveness of bees, tender against my skin.

THE PROMISE

What crowned gods are these that roam our streets,
invisible death squads, taking a toll of lives?
Placing my trust in hope, I carry on living, dreaming
of a world where hearts beat with compassion and minds
swim in rivers of light, rafting through rapids
of change, defying death, unclenching a fist,
claiming refuge in life, reaching for the sky.
Bound by laws of nature, gods do what they can
promising us the freedom to be ourselves—
treasured wrinkles on the face of a beloved,
a calligraphy of leaves against the light—
beauty unsurpassed, blossoming with age.
What reasonable person would choose to be a city
of demons, when you can be the metropolis of love?

BELIEVING

Believing you might appear disguised, I wait
with my prairie-open mind, let time and life
scatter my unknowing somewhere between faith
and doubt, mocking my need only the sky's emptiness
can fill, an emptiness where you should've been,
encouraging me to trust the passing clouds whose breaths
mist the looking glass of belief. The higher I climb,
poorer the visibility. Waiting for the dark to lift,
I sing in the half-light with insects of time buzzing
as I seek a sign, a mirror to see myself in, know
who I am. Are there journeys without destinations,
pilgrimages that don't lead to self-discovery?
May faith enter the interstices of doubt,
find fertile soil to put down roots, flower in.

STAYING ALIVE

I pray for the tide to turn, my grief and joy postpone.
Every day the news gets worse, I double my trust.
Even this will pass, I sigh, hanging on to hope.

Shocking the sight of empty shelves in supermarkets.
The extra fine veneer of civilisation stripped
in a heartbeat with talk of lives not worth saving.

The natural order of life is change, I reckon,
not forgetting it is darkest before dawn.
Singing in an uncertain world, I soldier on.

Believing in humanity, I keep an open mind—
pray for the hungry and homeless, ill and bereaved.
The death toll keeps rising all over the world.

Families bury their dead without ceremony.
For the frail and old abandoned in care homes,
death arrives masked as a saviour.

Not knowing when the pandemic will end,
I accept solitude as a path to staying alive—
the conversations with oneself necessary as ever.

In lockdown nature recovers, humans struggle—
our lives, in their reincarnations, unrecognisable.
Imagine the earth that was once a planet of trees.

NESTING

When her mobile beeped a message from GOV.UK—
New rules in force now: you must stay at home.
Protect the NHS. Save lives—shielding herself,

she enlisted to save lives, spent her days away
from friends and family, grateful they had homes
to shelter in. She had moved in with him the winter

before. When he went down on his knees
on Christmas Eve, she was over the moon. Setting
a date for marriage, she opened herself like a gift.

Never imagined life would take such a beating.
When he raided supermarkets, their home his ware-
house, she never questioned his manic buying spree.

The problem started after he was furloughed
and she had to work from home. He began to drink,
turned abusive unless she submitted to his every whim.

Her body, no more hers, was his plaything.
Broken and bruised, she could not eat, sleep, breathe—
her tears knew every synonym of fear and loathing.

Rescued by faith, her soul like a bird injured,
nesting in a knothole of the sky, took flight
to where every good thingness grew like trees.

STRANGE BEWILDERING TIME

Opening myself to life's mystery,
the foundation of my prayers, a daily thanksgiving—

my grief embraced all who died without a farewell,
none to hold their hand, no funeral, no vigil.

Fearing the random touch of fate I stayed home,
hoping to save lives. Every day the death toll rose—

each life precious in the mosaic of the universe—
I felt diminished as a human being.

Thinking of those struggling to survive,
unable to breathe, burning pyres stung my eyes.

It doesn't take much to make life bearable—
the hours wept, counting the cost of survival.

A deadly virus held a mirror up to society,
revealing the extent of our inhumanity.

Unless we make amends, change our reckless ways,
earth's treasures will disappear before our eyes,

leaving us at the edge of an abyss we cannot find
shelter in, in a world we cannot imagine.

Living in this strange bewildering time, the gift of
being human is a measure of who we can be.

I CAN'T BREATHE

In the middle of a once-in-a-lifetime
contagion, with thousands dead and thousands
more dying, unable to breathe, a video
of a killing goes viral, witnessed by a world
in lockdown, facing its hydra-headed demons,
unable to slay fears that keep multiplying.
In the clear light of day, in the land of the free
and home of the brave, under a sky that promises
freedom from cruel and unusual punishment,
a white policeman kneels, as if it was his
inalienable right, on the neck of a black
man, handcuffed, who keeps imploring:
I can't breathe, I cannot breathe, please I can't…
until he runs out of breath in the presence
of other police officers and bystanders
who record the execution, but do not intervene
to save the life of a fellow human being.
What hope is there for humanity if after
all this we fail to do the right thing,
remain voyeurs, spectators of violence and suffering,
wash our hands of centuries of injustice?

INSIDE ONE'S OWN SINGING

Selecting her own society, my soul
surrounds herself with truth and beauty—

garlands of exquisite memories
that wear their fragrance like gods and lovers

lost in an unimaginable shower
of grace, alight with the unbearable

pleasure of being here, steadying me
with the thought that whatever happens,

nothing is forever. Everything changes
when one has lived a long time alone.

Whether we know it or not,
we do not own the fruits of our actions.

We are as separate from our actions
as a decanter from the wine sparkling in it.

 If we accept the world as a gift,
  not take the gifts of the world for granted,

 we may learn to cherish what we have,
  thankful for things we never had, never needed.

We give according to our measure—
a steadfast prayer inside one's own singing.

PARADISE IN MY SOUL

Keen as a root quickening in darkness,
I was born to witness the world differently.

Wisdom of the universe centred in me,
I see what's hidden, discover what's forbidden.

In the astonishing light of my own being,
all that is dark turns bright as the sun.

Yet they call me stupid, moron, pugli—
a child who never grew up, not really.

Having survived so many knives carved
into me, edges sharp as inhumanity,

my pain earns invisible wings for bravery,
badges and medals, stars and ribbons of glory.

Carrying my own paradise in my soul
feels wicked. Breaking free, living like a god,

making my rules—flying, soaring, not forgetting
Icarus' fate, I consider myself touched, blessed.

Letting rip the madness, a river in spate
I open the doors to my infinite self—

much madness is divinest sense, a revelation—
an unexpected celebration, this Vishwarupa darshan.

WOKENESS

Lying awake all night examining this life,
an hour glass on the run, is no cure for jet lag.
Tossing and turning, an unusual homecoming
with street dogs howling, cats yowling,
the bellow of an insomniac bull, bone chilling—
a young female child's piercing cry shatters me.
In the land of my birth a woman is raped
every fifteen minutes. Shouldering the pain
and suffering of the world, night loses track of time.
Decades appear like yesterday—memory
of father dying, disappearing in a pyre of flames.
Never told him how much he meant to me.
How could I measure the continent of my loss
that keeps growing with the passage of time?
A car dodging potholes, horns blaring, jump-starts
me, disorienting as a plethora of roosters
cock-a-doodling-doo day and night without warning.
Accustomed to the muezzin's call to prayer
after the ecstatic dawn chorus that brings blessings
of sleep, this year's silence usurps my peace.
I wait all morning for the salawāt to begin.

WHAT OTHERS MAKE OF US

…for Sister St Michael

I

Transformed into a Trappist monk, I hang on—
a lay sister having gone to fetch her with the warning:

It could be a while, my dear, she tends to wander.
I imagine a Convent meditating on the Welsh border.

In a moment, I am a child in a rickshaw riding an elephant
on potholed roads. Mother's arm firmly strapped,

holding me tight as we journey into the unknown
to meet the Headmistress of St Joseph's Convent,

Cuttack, for the greater good of womankind.
It was my mother's mission to explain to Sister

with all the passion and reason she could muster
the importance of education and marriage to a woman.

To be married a graduate by eighteen was an insurance
against life's complex game of snakes and ladders.

My admiration soaring like a kite for the two women
in whose hands my fate hung evenly balanced.

A random roll of the dice and it could all be over
as it was for my mother when she was six. Losing a mother

is losing life's many gifts all at once—an education like no other
to be married and a mother twice over, all in her teens.

She could not find the words to impress on Sister
the need for a mother to do the right thing:

Everything is God's will. Daughters are precious—
she appealed to Sister, who barely a few years older,

sat listening intently as if at a confession,
knowing in her heart the world is illusion.

Understanding a mother's dilemma, Sister agreed
to a double promotion, my second in as many years.

And that is how I graduated at eighteen.
The marriage turned out to be a disaster.

II

Hello…a voice greets me like vespers,
bringing me back to the here and now.

An excited octave higher, I beam as if I had seen her:
How are you, Sister? Hope you are being looked after…

Her voice, revealing no sign of her four score and ten years,
echoes: How are you, my dear? How is your family?

Thinking she was asking about my mother,
it's that time of year when I visit my family in India—

I mention their visit to Highgate many summers ago
when my home echoed with their laughter.

How is your mother? She repeats as if I'd forgotten
to answer. Where do you live? What do you do?

I remind Sister of her beloved Convent in Cuttack,
tell her I've now lived in London longer

than in Cuttack, the place of my birth. Where is home,
I wonder as we play this game for a little bit longer.

How is your mother? Where do you live?
Are you working? How is your family?

Her memory ebbing and flowing—she forgets,
then remembers who she was when I first met her—

tells me things she's told me many times before.
I pretend it's the first time, patiently listen to her.

Time has a habit of rearranging the past—
and home's a place we've never been before.

We are not just what we make of ourselves—
we are also what others make of us.

LOOKING FOR MYSELF

A work of art, covering the face of agony,
ecstasy is fleeting, not universally shared.

Love may have a way of outlasting us,
change is our true companion in life.

Doubt plays a key part: like a child enters my heart,
wrecks everything I place my faith in.

The hours rarely pass without tiredness making
an appearance like the Chorus in a Greek tragedy.

Why did I think it normal to crawl on the floor
of the ocean of exhaustion, hoping for redemption

or the sky to provide me asylum in her kingdom?
Looking for myself among stars that lie shattered,

having donated their everything to the universe,
I discover the true meaning of altruism.

Living in a state of vulnerability, hanging on
to the tree of life sucking hope, each day a triumph

of improvisation, I pray for the chronically fatigued.
When doctors talk of asthenia, thalassaemia, genes and more,

I am in an IMAX movie theatre, watching an unreal world
exploding at its seam. How does one get at the truth?

Single, female, first generation immigrant, no security,
intelligent, neurodivergent, born to be different.

Don't they know that loneliness is a *cramping
of the spirit for lack of companionship*?

If only they knew the enterprise involved in finding
one's way through this universe of unknowing?

THE QUESTIONNAIRE

With a baking soda smile, she hands me
a clipboard as if it's the Rosetta Stone—

I mustn't drop it. And whispers, huskily:
Can you please fill this?

Place of birth, weight, nationality, ethnicity,
gender, how do you identify yourself?
Are you vegetarian? Do you suffer from insomnia?
How many hours do you exercise every week?
Do you have a partner, family, job, bank account?

So on and so bewildering…

After great struggle, I have reached a plateau
in the journey of my life—a place of neverlastingness,
where the universe, playing like *Air on the G string*,
offers me an alternative reality of things.

And, my mind wakes me up during my REM sleep,
raging against the injustices of our world—

its inhumanity, its wild and ferocious beauty,
its achingly irredeemable quality.

My answers want a universe of their own to spread their wings—

variations on a theme caught between a black-and-white
spectrum of invisibility, of attitude and collision,
playing hide-and-seek, doodling in the margins.

How does one respond to the last question, curious
and direct as a child: *Do you suffer from depression*?

THE WAITING ROOM

Joining the queue for a scan, we wait—
books on a trolley to be labelled, then shelved,
coloured spectrum of stories to be read.

Strangers, elbows touching, believing
all good things come to those who wait when
she whispered as if talking to herself:

One of the problems of growing old,
Isaiah Berlin once told Jeremy Paxman,
is not having any friends left to lunch with.

Unsure she was talking to me, I replied,
trying not to sound like Tina Turner:
What's age got to do with it?

When I first came here to study, I couldn't bear
to eat alone in my digs—bought the cheapest colour TV
for company. Back home, we had no TV—just family.

Yet the moment I placed a morsel in my mouth,
as if on cue starving faces from all over the world
appeared on my screen, haunting me through the day.

I began to lose weight. My doctor hospitalised me
puzzled by my body's grief of unknown origin.
Switching channels did not help nor heal.

The violence in our world is sickening—
even the Nature programmes leave me queasy.

We used to watch old movies, she intervened, nodding—
nostalgia spreading over her face like the blush of sunrise.
I still do, pretend my husband is here with me, holding my hand…

At that precise moment nurse entered, announcing
it would be a long wait: Why not take a break, refresh yourselves?
We have been refreshing ourselves since.

And I'm the one wondering who I'll lunch with as the world
keeps rearranging itself in ways unknown to me.

IF YOU LET YOURSELF BELIEVE

in the mystery of harmony, there being
no measure for such things. A need undefinable,

acquiring shape and meaning—not to fill
an emptiness, but a deepening of the spirit,

astonishing as a soul dwelling in two bodies,
representing a world. Trusted, generous, kind,

willing to listen—present in ways you can't imagine.
Life affirming as midwinter sunshine.

A blessing, unfolding like the birth of spring.
A wonder of creation, sustaining as nothing else can—

letting us see the best of what we can be,
a higher power if you let yourself believe.

Friends are precious, not just heirlooms—
they exist so we may see ourselves through their eyes.

Masterpieces of nature, disguised as weeds,
friends are not for display in look-at-me vases.

A garden sown with love's delight, friendship is
reaped over a lifetime of thanksgiving.

Conversations resume from where they were left off,
sometimes in silence more sympathetic than words—

not a nct cast forth with any design or purpose.
When the giving grows, the taking goes—

not following, nor leading; not judging, nor patronizing—
there being no better love than love, unquestioning.

THINKING OF YOU

I spend my days alone
thinking of you, our relationship,
trying to make sense of it.
Thinking of your limitless love,
I cannot recall when, where
or how I learnt of it. Are we born
with such a reckoning?
Hard are the days when I do not know
what to think, my world in pieces—
we're here because we're here because we're…
caught between faith and doubt.
How can we possibly know the things you keep
to yourself because that is your way?
Is it also part of your plan
to help me overcome the limitation
of being human? I've known
how easily lives are ruined,
seen the death of many a decent thing,
witnessed crimes and retributions
worse, spent lifetimes thinking about it,
emptied my mind of half-truths and lies—
embraced kindness, faith, gratitude,
humility, patience, hope—my guiding angels
protecting me from myself.
Human beings are willing to do anything,
some say they find it liberating.
I cannot find myself in this charnel pit,
prostrating to power, giving in to greed
and fear, blowing hatred out in destructive
bubbles. You made me different.
All I seek is a place in your temple
to sing. I've not given up on the possibility
of love. Nor have I given up on you,
my longing shining some days like the sun
for no reason except the joy of being.

SECRETS

To live in one's coppiced wilderness of secrets
takes a child's faith in the harness of secrets.

We are what we hide even from ourselves.
Who are we to judge the sinisterness of secrets?

Life may be an open book, yet gossip grows, turns
into strange creatures in the furnace of secrets.

When drumbeaters and axe-grinders take over,
they drown the world in the bitterness of secrets.

Know there are secrets—sacred and precious—
to be treasured in the foreverness of secrets.

There are things we don't know we know, unknown to us
their worth preserved in the ambergris of secrets.

A time comes when you can no longer remember
days disappearing in the tenderness of secrets.

To know and live with the secret of secrets is
peace, close as one gets to the innerness of secrets.

TASTE OF CHILDHOOD

My itinerant tongue never forgot the taste of childhood—

the piquancy of pineapple, notes of peach and pear
in jackfruit, burst of honey in mango, melon and lychee,

the tangy zest of tamarind, sweet aftertaste of sour amla,
bitter neem and karela, the astringent bite of jamun

in the tree-climbing, limb-bruising days of hide-and-seek,
eating guava, papaya, sapota. Digging for turmeric

in the sprawl of grandfather's grove facing the river,
bustling with wildlife, including a family of otters—

islands quivering with a siege of herons practising
their moves while you spent orgasmic afternoons sucking

mango, munching raisin, almond, and cashew,
waiting for a flash of kingfisher's indigo blue—

sipping nectar, sugarcane juice with salt and ginger,
swaying in a hammock from sturdy arms of nanny trees

when the world in your reach is for your pleasure,
ghar not mere bricks and mortar, but a state of belonging,

Vilayat, the vast unknown out there, beckoning—
and you a sapling born to stay put, not travel hopefully.

Who would've thought years later the sparkling laughter
of pomegranates would reduce you to tears,

or the ceremony of cracking open the hard exterior
carry you home to the tenderness of kernel in the belly

of green coconuts and the soft, scented pulp
of ripe wood apples, tree sprung from the sweat

of a goddess, its sacred leaves offered in worship,
transport you to the inner sanctum of temples?

Like oranges, apples, bananas, and grapes you make
a home of the world, holding your worlds together—

the place of your birth where all your efforts to escape
landed you in a place where all your attempts to belong

were thwarted, pointing to a world elsewhere, leaving
you in between, in a not-this-not-that state of being,

double helix of past and future wrapped round each other,
an afterwardsness, dancing to the music of the present.

This persistence of memory is no ordinary thing—
a lifeline like mother's milk, la dolce vita homecoming.

THIS IS WHERE WE LEARN WHAT IT MEANS TO BE HUMAN

Everything begins here, in the warmth of the rasoi,
where we learn to roll perfectly round rotis,
trace the map of the world on their phulka bodies.

A mandala where we meditate on life's meaning,
where gifts of the earth transformed by the alchemy
of love are miracles that resurrect us daily.

A rasoi is where we prepare food fit for gods.
This is where we learn what makes us who we are,
savour each other's cooking with an acquired taste.

A rasoi can be anything you want it to be—
a shelter in a storm, an umbrella in the scorching sun,
a place for the building of character, for thanksgiving.

Recipes are lives enriched in the service of others.
This is where we honour our ancestors: grandmothers'
creations are secret mantras we gift our daughters.

A place for remembering, conjuring, storytelling,
we are all transformed into stories, offered to deities.
A rasoi is where we can let ourselves be—

cherish the freedom of our thoughts, desires, destinies—
the chain of love holding our frayed selves together,
a place we keep returning to without fear of censure.

Thankful for our failures, our best teachers,
we learn failure is the stepping stone to success
and success the art of never giving up on our dreams.

Embracing imperfection, we explore paths that build
on tradition, leading to a wide open world of mystery,
where things happen in the secret inwardness of us.

We rejoice in the ecstasy of panch puran dancing
on a bed of chopped onions and curry leaves in a pan
touched with oil; not to mention the entanglement

of bay leaves, garam masala, garlic and ginger.
The ritual of sprinkling freshly chopped coriander,
strands of saffron, barks of cinnamon, folding love and desire.

This is where we share our dreams and fears, the reason
for our being here, resolve our quarrels in the togetherness of
being, celebrate the beginning of joyous things—

our apprehension, confusion, the shock of recognition
reconciled, recalling times past, lessons learnt, enmities forgiven.
This is where we learn what it means to be human.

DEPARTURES, ARRIVALS

I

A bustling island from where dreams travel
in an adrenaline rush of landing and takeoff.

Destinations, flight information, hopes and fears
cascading down information boards

remind me of children sliding down playground
slopes, screaming with exhilaration.

Laughter and tears, greetings and farewells
conjure sculptures and ornaments in an art gallery.

Two couples, one young, one not so young,
locked in embrace, kiss with unending passion.

A woman in maroon and blue, her face half veiled,
stands restless beside an older man in a crumpled suit.

In the next row a young woman with child
dressed in designer jeans, bejewelled, is lost in a book.

Nothing to suggest they might be related—
the young woman and the couple until they walk together

to the departure gate, pushing their trolleys in familial silence.
Like background music setting the scene in films

the public address system keeps announcing.
Glued to their mobile phones, no one listens.

II

Waiting at Baggage Claim I watch the theatre
of humanity unfolding as in an Advent calendar.

The conveyor belts move like waitresses,
balancing their heavy plates of hors d'œuvres—

suitcases of all dispositions and humour,
revolving like dishes in a Chinese restaurant.

Who would have guessed the colour
of skin, eyes, hair come in so many shades,

or human features cover a range
impressive as the mighty Himalayas?

Knowing no two humans are perfectly identical,
I keep an eye on the next revelation

as faces light up, smiling rainbows,
a rush of oxytocin worth waiting for.

Others practice to be patient, stand by for a sign,
a confirmation of love and forgiveness, compassion

and redemption, knowing we are nothing.
Yet out of nothing can come something precious.

Insignificant our days in transit unless
we take a measure of our lives, make a difference.

AGAINST THE ODDS

Days arrive with horizons of hope
as if God's smiling, urging the sea and sky
to deliver us home.

Trusting the elements to
take us there, we pray with a feeling of joy
when sudden disappointment comes.

Drifting flotsam, we witness lives lost by acts
of nature indifferent as the atrocities of men.

For how long can one fight against the odds,
seek a place to stand on to change the world—
let life take root somewhere one can call home?

It takes time to replenish faith, repair invisible wings.

The fears of the world are not of a constant
quantity, the sea of disappointment keeps rising.

Yet we take lives in our hands
sacrifice everything with the hope,
not promise, of landing on a safe shore—

thinking happiness is what we are born for,
why the sun rises to shine on our dreams
and suffering our unflinching guide.

NO LAND, NO HOME

...with acknowledgement to Mahmoud Darwish

Those who have no land, no home,
washed in like debris on a beach, imagine

not a painted ceiling, just a sky promising
nothing, not even the company of clouds.

Those who have no home, no land,
expect no welcoming ceremony, seek refuge

in exchange for life—dreams sealed in hearts,
names of loved ones dissolving under the tongue.

Those who have no land, no home,
have no hope that glimmers, no heaven

that illuminates—only the freedom
to die from longing and exile.

Those who have no home, no land,
tossed between unknowns, transformed

into stone, continue to believe in miracles,
trust in suffering to take them home.

Those who have no land, no home,
know what it means to be effaced—

shorn of a self, turned into a shadow, tired
of the fight, fearful of forgetting the way.

Only the wind listens to our secrets,
chatters at the edge of shivering coasts.

How can we thank the wind for revealing
the truth to the trees, sky, and seas—

a home, a home, a life for a home—
crying out for those who have no home?

IT HAPPENED

It happened, therefore it can happen again.
        ...Primo Levi

When it happens, remember it happened before.
It will happen again. We have a way of forgetting—

a form of self-preservation. Yet, memories breathe
in blood and bones, survive through generations.

Do not think it never happens to decent people
like you and me—ordinary, salt of the earth variety.

Perhaps the reason why you never heard of it.
Just because we never heard doesn't mean

it never happened. It happens all the time.
By the time we hear of it, it's rampant,

happening to everybody—some more famous
than we will ever be. It's never too late

to do something about it. It happened before,
it is happening now. It will happen again

with a different end or beginning.
That's just it, there's no way of knowing.

Do not presume it will not happen to you—
bad things often happen to good people.

Think of what you can do in the face of calamity,
not be overwhelmed by its immensity.

AFTERWORDSNESS

…on the 75th anniversary of India's Independence

Waking to a sky flushed with the colours of dawn,
I am a child, larking about free as a cloud.

In that pristine light one lived, hypnotised.
What did I know then of illusion and lies?

Childhood was home and the world was in my grasp.
Faith embraced doubt, contradictions lay side by side—

not soldiers slain in the battlefield of Kurukshetra,
where gods fought alongside men in the *Mahabharata*.

Did they not know that in war you kill or get killed?
The world may be illusion and the soul immortal—

call it what you will: inexperience or innocence,
we grew up believing in life, in values shared.

Compromise was an art perfected over centuries—
learnt from days ruled half and half by light and dark.

Behind open windows, curtains fluttered like prayer flags.
Freedom was a story that began at the beginning of time.

Independence a black and white film we watched,
spellbound. Old men said things we did not understand.

Actors in a silent movie, we were young, unprepared
to defend the history of a fabulously wealthy land.

A place renowned for her infinite treasures,
ransacked over centuries by her usurpers—

the last of her colonisers abandoned her in tatters,
carved her up in disgraceful haste, faithless arbitrators—

front gardens and backyards razed into no man's land,
millions made homeless, millions more massacred.

The violence and bloodletting, once unleashed,
rampaged like a blood thirsty tyrant unable to stop.

Hindus and Muslims, who'd lived together
for generations suddenly turned against each other.

Partition gave birth to retribution that spread like wildfire.
Forgiveness and compassion found a way of surviving too,

holding on like sacred grass unaware of worlds elsewhere.
Believers went out of their way to save strangers.

Liberation promised peace if not reconciliation.
It was time to rescue the wasteland from oblivion.

Shantih was on everyone's lips like a mantra,
long before I was a spark on the horizon.

Growing up, there was no inheritance to squander—
just a handful of hope and the prayers of ancestors.

Our elders, witnesses all, trusted in God—
knew words fall silent as they rise to meet the gods—

believed God and the Imagination are one,
and being together somewhere was blessing enough.

As I travel my own landscape of tears,
some beautiful as the Himalayas—

I learn what happens to us is not always in our hands,
nor are we the powers that shape our destiny.

The past lives on in the shadow of the future—
we mere innocent bystanders caught in the crossfire.

Sometimes, you lose everything you believe in.
Some wounds never heal, they bleed forever…

Who am I if not the embodiment of the past,
a way of life carved out of centuries of dreaming

not always according to our measure. Setting up
home beyond the seven seas, building bridges in space

and time, I keep an open house, furnish it with song—
invisible guests come in and out at will.

MOSCOW TO ST. PETERSBURG

Feeling mostly fury by the time we find the tail
of a queue snaking to the ticket booth,

unable to read the signs, speak the language,
amid the hustle and bustle, anxious to get on the train,

we are at breaking point. Finally aboard,
crisis averted we settle down, breathe deeply,

scan the compartment for a friendly face.
Our co-passengers in uniform are young, brash, tipsy.

No sign of a Tolstoy, Chekhov, Pushkin or Dostoevsky,
Akhmatova, Mandelstam, Pasternak or Tchaikovsky.

We fast forward through forests of stunning birch,
miles of white bark flushed in sunset-peach.

To pass the time we play a game—decipher names
of stations as landscapes, churches, silhouettes disappear

with the delicate dasvidaniya of leaves.
We pass Novgorod, moving uncertainly

towards the edge of a bloodied continent,
knowing not what to expect at our journey's end,

which feels like a beginning. Lighting fireworks
with history, the universe celebrates its immensity.

The orgasmic autumn sun sings its swan song—
asks why we keep destroying the earth's resources?

Do we not know we don't inherit the earth
from our ancestors, we borrow it from our children?

Is that why we seek to connect in new ways,
why journeys begin with true minds meeting?

IN A TIME OF SIEGE

…Paris: 13 November 2015

Moving to music in the concert hall, we shrugged
off gunshots, mistaking them for fireworks.

In an instant we got a grip on reality
as masked men sprayed bullets and blood.

Bodies bursting with life moments ago
like actors on a stage lay inert on the dance floor.

Except this was real, you sprawled on me,
protecting me with your last breath.

In the dark night of my soul I hear
screaming, wake up in a sweat, howling.

My days are locked in, incoherent with fear—
loneliness has usurped my peace, grief my cheer.

Where does all this hatred and violence come from?
Did they not arrive, dreaming of this land as their home?

Unbearable this poisoned shroud that keeps
diminishing my world to nothing.

Release me from this coffin that I may breathe,
not die longing for a sky to make me feel at home in.

SUNFLOWER SEEDS

My peace is shattered by the siren of an ambulance
in our street syncopating with air raid warnings
on TV as images of atrocities unfold in Ukraine.

The look on the wizened face of a man bent with age,
standing in the ruin that used to be his home,
his complaint addressed to the sky, his eyes asking: Why?

haunts me. Knowing the jungle lurks everywhere
does not make it easier to accept things as they are.

I have seen the splendours of Lviv and Kyiv—
the faith of worshippers in the Monastery of the Caves.

Those who believe, pray. Are you listening, God?   He doesn't exist
Those who can, promise to fight long as it takes.

Paranoid, drunk with power, a tyrant spreads
death and destruction, feeds the lives of fellow humans
like logs thrown into a train's furnace.

Truth may have many faces, but when it stares
me in the face, there is no escape. I cannot say—
there by the grace of God—and cross the street,

pretend Bosnia, Syria, Yemen, Afghanistan never happened:
nor Bucha, Borodyanka, Kherkiv, Mariupol…
The ghosts of Srebrenica, Grozny, Aleppo appear.   and Palestine?

The evening sky, glowing outside my window
in the colours of Ukraine, lends me strength to resist.

Knowing how it feels when left with no choice,
I accept vulnerability like a seed,
believe in life when buried in a black hole—

cannot stop thinking of sunflower seeds
an old lady gifted a young soldier defending her street.

FIND ME

In a child refugee's orphaned eyes, find me.
In the daily promise of sunrise, find me.

Soldiers rescue an old woman, a bag of bones
trapped in rubble, calling out to the skies: *Find me.*

Women and children disappear without a trace.
In their helpless, anguished cries, find me.

Surveying the desolation of ruined lives
in forsaken cities of grief the wind sighs, find me.

In voices rising from shallow graves, souls cry,
emerging like a flutter of butterflies, find me.

Unheard, unrepresented, they survive like seeds
praying in cracks of abandoned high-rise, find me.

In stories buried in the bones of exiles,
forgotten in the annals of history's lies, find me.

ALEPPO, MY ALEPPO!

My beloved city—
what have the barbarians done?

Once the beating heart of the world,
its flourishing trade routes,
the envy of nations, I lie in ruins.

My soul seeks peace. Instead I hear screams,
ghosts weeping in a giant graveyard.

I've been ruled by Hittites, Assyrians, Mongols,
Mamelukes, Ottomans, Arabs, and Greeks—

my city walls sheltered Christians, Kurds, Yazidis,
Turkomans, Armenians, Circassians—outsiders all.

Emperors had come and gone,
the splendour of my land had grown.

At the height of my glory the great mosque
was born, followed by the grand citadel,

palaces, souqs, madrasas, caravanserais,
castles, churches, libraries, museums, monasteries.

I survived bullet holes lodged in the flanks
of my imposing Roman walls—

the beauty of my rich Byzantine churches,
mosques and crusader fortresses.

Never imagined my magnificent monuments
would be reduced to rubble, my proud people
forced to flee, seek refuge in strange lands.

Those who stayed live in fear,
in streets that stink like slaughterhouses.

Parched without water the weakest go first,
orphaned children die, playing with cluster bombs.

No one knows how many perished in this war,
how many fled leaving their possessions—
every family broken, severed.

Can this be the will of Allah?
lamented the ghost of the ancient city of Aleppo.

What is left to squabble over—
not riches, nor honour? It's not power

that brings freedom, only love for all creation.
Every son and daughter of Aleppo knows this truth.

Did they all die in vain defending the faith,
their souls locked in this godforsaken city?

Where have my thriving enterprises gone,
my craftsmen, goldsmiths, mapmakers, glassblowers?

My libraries, museums, coffee houses, schools—
the home of explorers, inventors, the brave, and curious.

There is no debate, dance, music or muwashshah—
all I hear is the deafening blast of missiles and bombs.

Where are my scented gardens and fountains,
when will I hear bird song and laughter of children,
lose myself in a whiff of jasmine?

VIEW FROM THE GODS

Didn't you say nothing will come of nothing—
was it then wise to strip yourself of everything?

There's no love nor rest in nothingness,
taking upon yourself the mystery of things—

many more ways to learn *unaccommodated man
is no more but such a poor, bare, forked animal…*

That is how we are deceived,
mistaking our limits for that of others.

Dreaming of impossible things,
we place our trust in those undeserving.

I am no more the mistress of my life
than you mighty King were of yours.

Owning nothing but myself, my powerlessness
cannot buy my rightful place in this playhouse.

Arriving alone, dispossessed, I take my seat in the gods,
witness men unleash the terrors of the earth.

Living at the edge of any universe also serves a purpose—
the view from the gods is no less precious.

THE RECKONING

The first thing I notice is his face, glowing—
the whiteness of his robe enhancing

his dark, mesmerising gaze, unnerving,
yet calm in the face of calamity. Stepping

out of the claustrophobic frame, away
from the menacing grip of mocking men,

he carries on the conversation he began
centuries past. Holding my attention,

timeless its provocation, the implicit question:
Who are you, what manner of human are you?

Surrounded by tormentors, dressed to kill,
men who are not fit to worship at his feet—

false prophets, preening hypocrites, torturers,
bullies and connivers, undeserving of his gift.

One in a flamboyant hat sporting a sprig of oak,
the acorn in its cup winking like solid gold,

his throttling dog collar with shiny spikes speaks
of misplaced loyalty to his paymaster, not his redeemer.

Another balances a wreath of thorns on his head
while an iron gauntlet protects a perfidious arm.

A belligerent arrow wrapped in the green folds
of his fashionable headgear leaves me squirming.

The third man with white hair and spiky goatee beard,
a crescent moon and yellow star on his flowing

headdress, stands leering as one molesting hand
rests presumptuously on Christ's body. The fourth

leans forward, hands raised to uncover Christ's robe—
schadenfreude written large on their louring faces.

I'm left meditating on loneliness and suffering,
measuring what manner of human I am, have been.

CHANGE

I despair when I look out, see no hope for change—
tell myself, be patient, there's always scope for change.

The only constant in our capricious world,
it's nature's promissory note, a horoscope for change.

Time takes her toll giving birth to change. We appear
briefly glorious in life's kaleidoscope of change.

It may be easier to change myself than the world.
No harm leaving prayers in love's envelope for change.

If greed and ignorance, pride and power are here to stay,
practise being a hermit, not a misanthrope, for a change.

When nothing works, I surrender with grace to change,
pretend being a gazelle or an antelope for a change.

I no longer despair when I look in, see no scope for change—
tell myself: Shanta, be patient, there's always hope for change.

EXILE

Alien, outsider, firangi, gaijin, exile—
are some names of the pariah gods of exile.

Once exiled, always an exile; no place to call home—
a stranger in a strange land, speaking in tongues of exile.

You learn to stand alone, commit your faith to luck—
a roll of the dice, the random walk of exile.

All your efforts to belong somewhere thwarted
by shadows that darken your life in exile.

Across the world people dream of home and belonging,
not to uproot themselves for a lifetime of exile.

A state of mind, it is the freedom to die
in a world elsewhere from the loneliness of exile.

You offer yourself, your treasures, knowing the world
is enriched with the toil and tears of exile.

Only to see your life's work destroyed, unacknowledged,
not rise like prayers in grand cathedrals of exile.

Your thunder stolen, you rail within, ask the sky
why there is no justice for the grief of exile?

The earth blesses all migrations. They say God roams
the streets disguised in tattered robes of exile.

If you have no eyes to see I am human, feel my heart
beat with the compassion of one in self-exile.

May peace and enlightenment be yours, my soul—
Vilayat's music can only be heard in exile.

SOMEWHERE TO COME HOME TO
...for Mimi Khalvati

She makes entries on light in white ink,
hieroglyphics in the womb of the Sphinx.

When she turns to mirror work,
reflecting a tapestry of water,
higher flies the thought, more rarefied its air.

It makes you long for the world,
        take a lungful of pleasure
so that sated you turn, blot out the world
        enter another, settle for words.

In the doorway stands a poem—
her signature is everywhere
among galaxies, infinities: an incredulity
that leads even infidels to prayer.

You join in her wishes that words were inks,
        inks quills for lyres,
lyres space lattices for broken narratives—
childhood mountain cities left behind.

And for those who have no crook in the road
to mark their winding route,
no chine cleaving the mind in two, a line
on the land's belly, let her song serve
        as a stopping-inn, an open invitation,
somewhere to come home to, a sky to feel alone in.

BETWEEN THOUGHTS
...for Hugo Williams

Don't look down, hold exact location
of your life within a single action.

Face against the sun, famous in that air,
you can see every leaf, life from up there.

Accidents will happen, smiles turn into frowns
as your words go crashing down among the clowns.

You sharpen your faculties once more
covered with sentences, images of lovers galore—
watch yourself, no more stage struck, unlocking a door.

Right moments as you know don't happen
if wrong ones are never taken.

The best in us is what we do in an
emergency, not later seeking clemency.

Forced to find faith in a crisis,
open yourself to poetry like passion,
the instinct of a jackal following his lion.

For that is happiness: to wander alone facing one's self,
not one's reflection rising from the brilliance of surfaces.

Accepting loss, becoming part of a stillness,
lost among the submarine silence

of stones, ghosts of temples shining perfect,
when time runs out on you, and you are too late,
caught between featureless and the infinite,

to shut the cupboard that contains the sea;
the ancient symbols of fortune on your blanket your key.

You disappear into the desert of dreamtime
knowing what manner of a human you have been.

HEARING EYE

...in memory of John Rety

Turning to poetry when all your paintings were stolen,
you discovered what's hidden in words.

Living between languages in the company of poets,
you went where the willow washed her syllables.

Losing a country you gained an empire,
began to resemble an archangel with the flight of time—

high priest of poetry, master of ceremonies,
your songs of anarchy, shining stars, lit up the sky.

No more a stranger in a strange country, you were
as much at home with hecklers and furry creatures,

welcoming all to your durbar—your namaste
like a sorcerer's arc greeting me with *Not This, Not That.*

An angel dancing at the crossroads, you blessed poetry—
all came to you—words in search of poets,

poets in search of a hearing eye.
Your sympathetic eye heard prophecies

of sleeping volcanoes, a nine fold of charms,
a Prague winter. You showed us how to see, hear,
live at the edge without fear, reminding us:

The most we can hope for
is that we might be understood by others
with different understandings
to ourselves.

GOING HOME

Unable to find my way home,
the way back, also the way forward,
is suddenly no longer the same.

Not the way leaves change the look of widowed
branches winter-bare, and trees spring-green alter
the neighbourhood into a celebration of life—

the landscape of my dreams is surreally transformed.

The return journey from my local corner shop,
familiar to me as the back of my hand,
unrecognisable as I emerge with the day's newspaper.

The bobby-on-the-beat, whom I've never
met before, greets me, and says he knows where I live—
takes me to Buckingham Palace without word or ceremony.

A stranger in a strange land, I am home,
real as in a dream, nothing seems the same any more—
not the past, present, not the future.

The world is crazier than we reckon.
I join the Royal family and mine huddled together,
eating out of tupperware, watching television.

BE THE GODS

It took all the gods to make her invincible.

Offering their radiance, each contributed to her
magnificence, bestowing her with the power

to protect and destroy. Her spirit, the supreme union
of divine forces conjured to destroy evil that threatened

the gods—a ritual celebrated every year to remove
suffering on earth, suffering born of human frailty.

It took all the gods to conceive of such a deity
just as *it takes a village to raise a child*.

Until the village embraces every child as precious,
daughters like sons, gifts of the universe—

until such time we learn to mend ourselves,
be the change we want to see in others,

we cannot overcome the injustices of our world
vulnerable to all manner of inhumanity.

We are what we make of ourselves; we are also
what others make us. Be the gods that made Durga.

OF GODS AND GODDESSES

Brightly coloured posters of gods and goddesses
bathe in the light as rising spirals of incense

mingle with the scent of muskmelons in the market-
place. Arcs of desire bouncing behind bodices

distract from the arcane business of the day—
the purchase of perfectly ripe melons and lemons.

Luscious the sway of hips of heavenly creatures
with the look of flowers upon their faces.

Irresistible the rush of hormones, pheromones
when the body acquires a mind of its own.

Thrown into a state of confusion, a young man
possessed by an irrepressible hunger

bends forward, legs crossing, recrossing, half kneeling
to redeem himself, smelling the lemons stacked

pyramid-like, serendipitously on shelves, providing
the cover he needed. Reviving from his fainting

spell, the world in his hands, defying gravity,
he inhabits the heady aura of gods and goddesses.

MEETING *LE RÊVE* AT THE TATE MODERN

Slouched in an armchair in a sculptural
arrangement of surreal shapes, seductive

the lift of her left breast revealing a sensuous
body, face resting on her right shoulder,

eyes closed in abandonment, her features
aligned, not portrayed haphazardly—

the eyes to the right, the nose to the left.
For an instant I am inside her dreams.

The strong lines of her fingers draw attention
to her crotch, nudging me to reassemble

the pieces; and before I am aware of it
the distorted face falls into place as my eyes

refocus and the half crescent of her eye
morphs into a foreskin, and try as I might

I can't unsee the erection embracing her face
in this exhibition of love, fame, and tragedy.

Two silver-haired ladies in gold-rimmed glasses
stagger in on crutches, applauding: *lovely, lovely*—

taken in by the colours from a distance.
A gaggle of schoolgirls scatter in stitches.

SHE REMEMBERS

It was the day of our swayamvara—
celebration of a love that could not be named.

Dressed like queens we sat on royal chariots
gilded for the occasion, returning home victorious—

his sixteen thousand and hundred wives
to be precise—our faces blooming like lotuses.

The palace was live with music, dance, fireworks,
heady with the fragrance of frankincense and brahma kamala.

A beam of truth, Satyabhama, Krishna's third consort,
helped to wage war against that god-turned-demon

who kept us hostage for years. It was her arrow
that killed Naraka, saving the sisterhood strong as love.

We no longer had homes to return to, discarded
by our families, husbands, and in-laws as damaged goods.

None of us being Sita, it was not trial by fire
we were destined for, but a life of great tribulation.

Marriage saved us from dishonour and death.
How could we not have lost our hearts to Krishna?

Young and besotted, we dedicated our lives
to Govinda—a choice we had made individually

to belong to no man other than Krishna.
Women in love do things others cannot fathom.

We wanted him to do to us what he did with music—
driving his devotees to ecstasy with his flute.

That full moon night we longed to be possessed by him.
I could have sworn he spent the night with me.

A woman reborn, I was in a cloud of wonder
when a radiant Radha confessed the morning after

that they had spent a night of passion together.
It made me jealous, Radha's innocent banter.

Echoes of amorous songs and wild laughter
washed over me before I reached the banks of the river

where gopis, consorts of Krishna, gossiped,
their supple bodies glowing with pleasure.

Like charged particles drawn to a magnet,
our hearts beat faster when he entered our thoughts—

we moved irresistibly towards him, our lover and
redeemer, attracted by more than his beautiful body.

His eyes could read the calligraphy of true desire,
every pore of his dusky blue, thundercloud skin

singing with the rapture of one who surrenders.
His hair the entanglement of the universe.

In the ocean of love there are no borders,
love mints its image everywhere.

Those who do not know such joy could never
have guessed its origin, what it means to be in heaven.

We ignored gossipmongers, there were many—
such bliss, unreservedly bestowed, was ours to savour.

The scent of sandalwood, jasmine, and lotus
rose from our bodies, swelling waves in high tide—

like worshippers we entered each other's caves,
passion lighting the path to our inner sanctums

as we abandoned ourselves to savour orgasmic nectar.
In those nameless moments we were all existence.

WARRAMABA VIRGO

Day the right of a woman to her body was overturned
in the second largest flawed democracy of the world,

I was in bed nursing a cold, listening to the news, thinking
nothing can surprise me any more when a passing mention

caught my attention—the existence of uniquely efficient,
independent, parthenogenetic females who've changed

the rules in their favour. Cloning themselves for over
thousands of years without any disadvantage to their

wellbeing, these rare creatures dispensed with the male
of the species altogether, taking refuge in each other.

Producing twice as many eggs as their sexual counter-
parts, these intelligent, celibate, green, slender

as matchsticks, grasshoppers do not mate to fertilise
their eggs, reducing the risk of predation—

knowing there isn't enough ecstasy to compensate
for the agony of finding and keeping a sexual partner.

This miracle they seem to have achieved, thriving
merely on mulga acacia, on shrubs and bushes,

savouring a keen and contrary sense of humour
in the traditionally macho mining areas of Broken Hill.

What a wonderful world…wafted in through my window.
Lost in the possibilities of Satchmo, I couldn't help imagine

a world full of wonder where the odds of becoming
pregnant was balanced evenly between the sexes.

THE TREE HUGGERS

*…in memory of Amrita Devi, her three daughters along with the men
and women of the Bishnois community who were martyred in Khejarli,
Rajasthan, in 1730*

When soldiers came to cut down the trees for wood to build the
Maharaja's palace—

trees that were paths to universes beyond reckoning,
the feet of gods, lifeblood of the village,
trees that had been there from the beginning of memory,
immortalised in the *Mahabharata*,
trees they worshipped, sheltered under the shamiana
of their venerable branches, where promises
were made and dreams fluttered like prayer flags,
trees that were sacred texts defining their dharma…

Unable to bear witness to the devastation of their way of life,
drenched in faith, hugging a tree, she cried out to the soldiers
          on horseback:

This soil is ours, this water and air ours,
ours are these trees, the splendour of our villages,
our shringara, gifted to us by our ancestors,
a legacy for generations to come…
You have to kill me first before you kill this tree—
a chopped head is cheaper than a felled tree.

She saw the sky fall through the branches as soldiers axed her and
her daughters—each clinging to a khejri, joined in protest.

The king's horses reared up as the earth turned red.
Blackbucks, their spiral horns sticking out in dissent,
skittered with the gazelles, partridges, and quails.

The wind gods carried their message to neighbouring
villages—old and young, women and men, rich and poor—
rushed to save their priceless possessions.

Holding on to courage and compassion,
each embraced a tree, humming and singing together,
refusing to let go until one by one,
they were beheaded by the Maharaja's soldiers.

GOING NOWHERE

…for Joy Harjo

In my dream I'm lost, unable to return home. The way back, which is also the way forward, is no longer the same—not the way flowers change the look of a tree and trees alter the neighbourhood. Home is a tree spreading her roots everywhere, going nowhere.

When I wake up, it's a blessing to find myself in bed staring at familiar presences, almost a joy to know one hasn't been lost anywhere. I'm where I am supposed to be—at home, going nowhere.

Later, in the street, a stranger asks where I was going as if wishing me good morning. I nod, absentmindedly, say just out for some air, going nowhere.

Going somewhere is hard to negotiate. It could involve a fork in the road with a fifty percent chance of making the wrong choice, getting lost, going nowhere.

To fatten on branches and fall like a ruddy apple in an orchard, buried in the earth as the world keeps going the way of dinosaurs is one way of going nowhere. Better to let the universe choose you, so you can be properly lost finding yourself, going nowhere.

Dreaming of a new world blowing away injustice is a flock of clouds going God-knows-where. When those men raped and killed an innocent young girl, people marched down looted streets of dreams. I joined them in my grief, thinking we were going somewhere, not knowing we were going nowhere.

I have found myself in strange places where people gather to hear and share lies, where books fly from faithless hands as they buy and sell prizes. Not for the honest, the ruthless bidding. The brainless confer titles, the shameless accept them with that distant look in their eyes, knowing they were going nowhere.

Walking down a dirt path, I find myself in a field with a murder of scarecrows hanging about like nobodies, reassuring me I was going nowhere.

On the road to nowhere I meet a goddess and her ruined millionaire. They say they were doing nothing in the middle of nowhere. Going nowhere is a blessing, they said.

Living in a rainbow of possibilities, turning to the sky and heavenly bodies, who watched over me when I was born, I ask them where home was. I ask the trees and the rivers flowing like arteries, carrying the stories of my past and future lives. They tell me home is in your heart, you will know when you get there on your way to nowhere.

SONG OF PRAISE

…from prayers in different traditions

Praise the stars in their constellations
for knowing their place, yet blessing all migrations.

Praise the sun, powerful, yet unwavering
in its journey across the sky, light pulsing
through clouds, mists—life sustaining.

Praise the moon always true, waxing waning,
constant in its daily transformation.

Praise the earth as it moves on its axis—
inner and outer cores holding on to each other,
partners on the dance floor, steady as they go.

Praise day and night, mere limits of our perception;
and death, a release from our earthbound vision.

Praise the sky, air, ether; praise the universe
for awakening us to worlds beyond our imagination.

Praise water in all its forms, giving and taking—
blood flowing through continents of bodies.

Praise plants sun-facing, light-changing,
breathing in carbon, green deities in meditation,
giving us oxygen, expecting nothing in return.

Praise the eye of the guest—clear, observant.
Praise the giver of life—almighty, benevolent.

Praise every species in our planet,
masterpieces of evolution—
rich, rare, wild, keepers of infinite secrets.

ALWAYS BEGINNING

To see the universe with new eyes, not blinded by shadows light casts.
To find the resolve to be always beginning, never lose heart—
let the angels in, be open to perfection that never lasts.
In time everything changes, even our perception of truth.

To find the resolve to be always beginning, never lose heart—
to listen to the laughter of children opening up the sky.
In time everything changes, even our perception of truth.
Everything that is born dies, unknown to us the hereafter.

To listen to the laughter of children opening up the sky—
to connect to the universe with every breath of ours.
Everything that is born dies, unknown to us the hereafter.
Is there something somewhere patiently recreating us?

To connect to the universe with every breath of ours—
to rise like the sun when we fall, lose everything, almost.
Is there something somewhere patiently recreating us,
urging us to find the resolve to be always beginning?

To rise like the sun when we fall, lose everything, almost—
to keep an open mind, dream of meadows wild with flowers,
urging us to find the resolve to be always beginning.
It is to love we keep returning, the place with miraculous powers.

To keep an open mind, dream of meadows wild with flowers—
to risk everything for that heaven-on-earth feeling.
It is to love we keep returning, the place with miraculous powers.
Along the way we rise like a prayer, receive the world's blessing.

To risk everything for that heaven-on-earth feeling—
let the angels in, be open to perfection that never lasts.
Along the way we rise like a prayer, receive the world's blessing.
To see the universe with new eyes, not blinded by shadows light casts.

IF

If the universe had not been Love's creation,
life and light born in an unimaginable explosion—
                    we would not exist.

If the Milky Way and the dust of dying stars
did not scatter in space, in love's reincarnation—
                    we would not exist.

If the sun and moon did not send their rays to earth,
awakening us to worlds beyond our imagination—
                    we would not exist.

If our sky did not gift us with the gods of weather,
protecting us from space debris and radiation—
                    we would not exist.

If our planet did not revolve round its axis,
inner and outer cores locked in lovers' passion—
                    we would not exist.

If day and night did not daily renew their vows,
blessing us with light and darkness for our preservation—
                    we would not exist.

If water did not enthral us with the miracle
of creation, the beginning of life and evolution—
                    we would not exist.

If plants did not produce oxygen for no reason
except the pure joy of breathing in carbon—
                    we would not exist.

If every species did not have a purpose for being
here, their lives worthy of celebration—
                    we would not exist.

If nature's bounty and resilience did not go about
scattering the seeds of hope and compassion—
                            we would not exist.

If greed and ignorance, pride and power
stand in the path of enlightenment and realisation—
                            we will cease to exist.

GRANT US

Grant us the wisdom to survive
like trees that live long, enriching the planet—
loyal protectors of the realm, standing firm,
asking for nothing in return of heaven or earth.

Grant us the wisdom to imagine
like oysters transforming grit into pearl—
the need to give and forgive, not merely receive,
the giving growing, becoming something precious.

Grant us the wisdom to rejoice
a long time after we are returned to earth that the lives
we leave behind may cherish the fruits of our action—
a million species saved from extinction.

Grant us the wisdom to love—
love without limit, love that casts a widening
circle of light for the world to walk forward in,
singing the songs of its forgotten stories.

Grant us the wisdom to pray—
pray to set right the injustices we perpetuate,
courage to change the things that must be changed,
else there will be nothing left to live for.

FROM THE BOOK OF TRANSFORMATIONS

Her dreaming, transformation—
call it what you will—protects us:
      imperceptible her becoming…
Circling in her orbit, the earth bears the scars
of creations, extinctions, resurrections.

Altering her course many times
before entering the sea, trembling
with fear and excitement of losing
her identity and gaining that of the ocean—
even a mighty river is a child entering the world.

Trees stand astonished at the inability
of humans to mend while they renew themselves
effortlessly, year after year,
remembering the earth as a planet of trees
and humans rare as blue moon sightings.

The moon sends images of her many selves,
letting it sink in she is not what meets the eye—
      mysterious her origin…
the stars hum in a chorus, acknowledging change
is the only steady state, death a transfiguration like no other.

Winds gather intelligence from every leaf and flower,
hear every prayer lost in skies of grief,
know every injustice leads to retribution—
air, water, fire, earth share their wisdom, urging us
to learn the secret language of the universe.

Rainbows chant *make me always the same as I am now*—
seasons keep changing the view from my window.
      The soul is a lonely wanderer…
In the book of transformations, the next episode
is being written. I change my world by changing myself.

CONTRARINESS OF BEING

When I reconcile myself to the randomness
of the universe, everything falls into place.
Except the trees outside my window sigh with the wind—

The laws of nature cannot be arbitrarily bent.
To be a tree is profound responsibility.
The moon smiles and says: *Try being me…*

In an uncertain world, I reason, my life
cannot possibly have any special purpose?
Unexpectedly, the meaning of life is revealed to me.

The opposite of a great truth is also a great truth—
I hold the thought like aerial roots of banyan trees.
The god of small truths throws me into confusion.

When I accept I would never be fully understood
or loved, I am suddenly inundated with suitors.
Just when I think I'd found someone to hold on to,

I'm left with a turncoat revealing his true colours.
When love turns out to be another illusion,
like a blinding headlight, truth comes straight at me,

without any explanation, shattering everything I believe in.
After great struggle, I realise nothing is as it seems
when reality bursts at its seams, beckoning me

to participate in the dance, not observe from the margins.
A dervish in a trance, summer keeps me enthralled
until autumn arrives in all her splendour,

filling my days with rainbows of hope and laughter.
When I reckon the good times are here to stay,
winter leads me to the dark night of the soul—

covering my sky with vast clouds of unknowing.
Changed by suffering, I surrender to Life,
think mine must have come to an end

when I find myself in a world without end…

SOUL FEATHERS

—a bud, a beginning, a kiss, a promise,
an entire lifetime suspended in bliss—

—a feeling, cloud with a silver lining,
shining, unwilling to be diminished—

—always trusting, a child's grasp, five fingers
folded on a rainbow of dreams—

—a seed, an atom, an idea, a prayer,
dawn that dispels the nightmare—

—the common flower's eternal surprise,
springing in the cracks of cemented high-rise—

—a tree with branches bare, a solitary leaf waving,
not falling—snowdrops, crocuses, bluebells dancing—

—life hanging by a thread, street artist walking on air,
friend of faith and charity, enemy of fear and despair—

—the cry of a new born child rising like a white dove
with olive branch in an underground bomb shelter—

—a prisoner's solace, death's companion
the miserable person's medicine—

—an opened gift box and all that's left within—

INSTINCT

—reefs sway in all their splendour,
forests of filigreed corals pulsing with colour—

—reclusive creatures, neither plant nor animal
in caves, canyons, valleys of the deep in thrall—

—male seahorses flee, flashing trails of amber,
sharing secrets we are slow to decipher—

—giant arapaima swim among piranhas,
their mineralised scales a massive shield—

—dolphins with X-ray vision, peer
inside the stomach of sharks just for a laugh—

—catfish, big swinging tongue, taste prey from afar,
colossal squids digest food with their brains—

—seaweeds sigh when air rushes into their fold,
sea serpents soar on tides, bodies streamlined—

—turtles, octopi, starfish, sea urchins, jellyfish,
even the modest plankton displays a mind of its own—

—dragonfish hunt in the inky depths of seas,
submarine volcanoes light a ring of fire—

—the ebb and flow of waves and tides is nothing
but energy passing through water, unceasing—

—creation offers a fleeting vision of perfection,
the innocence and purity, the resilience of instinct—

SOLITUDE

Finding myself in this paradise of solitude,
I discover continents in the embrace of solitude.

Shafts of sunlight, startled by the beauty of gods
displaced, play in sacred spaces of solitude.

Their meditation disturbed not by devotees,
but strangers seeking the solace of solitude.

When everything you believed in turns to nothing,
be the light that burns with the grace of solitude.

At the still centre of being, this yearning is grief
for lives we cannot resurrect to trace solitude.

The overtakelessness of suffering is heartache—
the poetry of life written to efface solitude.

Life and death, the beyondness and afterwardsness,
are tricks of perception, the carapace of solitude.

A not-this-not-that awareness of the self can only
be realised in blessed terraces of solitude.

After such reckoning, what is life but prayer—
a crowning in the grand palace of solitude.

Not a cramping of the spirit, but a flowering
of the soul in life's rich pomace of solitude.

Divinity is in all this, is one with all that lives.
Know the world will leave you breathless for solitude.

Beneath it all the desire to love, be loved—
may you be found, gift-wrapped, in your lace of solitude.

When gods speak, they sing of truth and love,
peace and light—the infinite riches of solitude.

SNOWY EGRET

Smeared in ash, head bent in the morning mist,
one leg crooked, resembling an Indian yogi,

the snowy egret meditates beyond regret
and desire on the struggle to assuage hunger.

Perched on a boulder at the edge of the river
that keeps retreating every season, he waits—

a seasoned fisherman poised for a catch,
for a taste of flesh to freshen his mouth fouled

by plastic. Suddenly, he darts forward, dives in,
scoops a mouthful of quivering silvers.

Standing upright he savours the moment,
rapt in the dazzling company of clouds.

Lifting a creel of sunshine, he spreads his wings
with the grace of a ballet dancer disappearing—

immersed in his flight, one with the light,
soaring with the wind to the call of the universe.

CAMDEN VISITOR MOORINGS

The end of a perfect summer's day—
we ramble down the canal path, past Pirate Castle

and the shopping arcade where confetti sale signs
camouflage lives mired in quiet desperation.

Harassed shoppers go about their business,
wearing their mask of disappointments discreetly.

Everybody is dreaming of being somebody,
preparing to be chosen, immortalized for eternity.

Admiring the moored boats, we move along the track.
Suddenly, we are in the presence of five stunning villas—

Ionic, Veneto, Gothic, Corinthian, Tuscan—
already celebrated, recorded for posterity.

The water in the canal does not stop to consider
the inequities of our world. Unaware of its separateness,

it is one with the sunlight dancing on its surface,
lost in the moment's magical forgetfulness.

Birds, insects shimmy out and dazzle, pushing invisible
boundaries. Fish peer through the golden purdah,

mouths wide open gulping the day,
marvel at this illuminated cathedral of nature.

IT IS

It is the singularity of black holes
a swarm of hummingbird hawk moths
the insatiable hunger of caterpillars
smile of a camel, song of a nightingale
the moon frail as the edge of a fingernail—

It is dirty as a clam, economical as ants
dark as a pocket, convenient as money
nervous as a squirrel, close as a box turtle
an ostentation of peacocks, a siege of herons—

It is hardy as grass, fragile as a tiger
words sleeping between the covers of a book
a fanatic hiding his doubt, a sceptic his faith—

It is an unkindness of ravens, an exaltation of larks, the
spitefulness of philanthropists, a plague of poets—

It is none of the above.

I DO NOT KNOW WHAT IT IS

—this yearning for life, love, light,
an undying desire to make something beautiful of It—

love like a calligraphy of murmurations
the hum of ecstasy, songs that might survive
a flicker of the divine
the universe cradled in cosmic dust
birdsong inside the egg
waking to dawn chorus, feeling It—

It that is everything and nothing—
the wonder that is life, a precious gift
the silence in which others sing
the witchery of living, the magic of loving
when giving is receiving and knows It—

It is the strength to accept reversals—
spider's web fluttering like a prayer flag in the storm
trusting there is mystery beyond our reckoning
the astonishing steadfastness of trees
a willingness to learn from the promise
of life to be always beginning—

the wisdom to change the way we see things—
listen, be kind, humble, sparkle like fireflies
dancing in the night, drunk with delight
swimming naked in the river of imagination
the home of all our longing, belonging
choosing to live in that which is yes
which is infinite, in love's plenitude, in It…

It that is it and it and not it…

A PLACE OF AWARENESS

Slow to learn, we are bound to be in many minds
when disasters strike us. As our existential

crisis deepens, we can't imagine your existence
or the reason for ours. Every crisis may appear

inevitable in hindsight, it's clear as daylight
what matters is foresight. Compared to the history

of the earth, our climate is benign—a goldilocks scenario,
almost. A planet surrounded by dying stars, an asteroid

may one day lead us down the path of dinosaurs.
You may have other homes, dear Life, the earth is our

one and only. Our history one of migration and extinction.
We call it civilisation, the rise and fall of being human.

Knowing I do not know what I don't know,
not knowing what to believe in is no consolation.

Is *Know Thyself* one of your existential curveballs
and spin an essential aspect of your mission?

I watch on TV a crocodile bury her eggs in the sand
with the love and devotion of a human.

She guards them fiercely—alone, a single mother,
unable to fight off predators who feast on her unborn.

Squirming like a moth in the jaws of a lizard, I feel her
vulnerability. For Life to exist, God must too, I reckon—

not the gods of our past or present, not the ones we can
name—but One, undefinable, born from the gut of our doubt

and despair, grief and struggle, faith and compassion,
not to be worshipped, but to love and be loved—

abiding with us in our time of tribulation,
guiding us to a place of awareness, our exaltation.

THINGS

Inside each one of us are galaxies of things
known only to the God of infinite things.

There are universes we know nothing about,
enough to know we don't know a myriad things.

The journey within is vast as the one without—
even Time is not the ultimate arbiter of all things.

Life may end when external forces destroy us,
breaking free from within is the start of new things.

Webb, more powerful than Hubble, wanders in space
to catch the blinding light at the beginning of things.

Illusion is real, alters the way we see things—
the mystery and majesty, the dark energy of things.

Wisdom is keeping our minds open to all manner
of things—dark matter, cryptos, I-have-no-idea things.

No point thinking we are masters of the universe,
gods of the real and virtual worlds of things.

We are no such thing. In the beginning there was Love—
the Love we have forgotten in our love of things.

Nothing may have caused the Big Bang. Nothing.
It is possible the universe was born of divine things.

Imagine the joy when you renounce a confusion of things,
the freedom of I-don't-know-what-to-believe-in things.

No more eclipsed by the long shadow of things,
you find yourself on top of a Himalaya of nothings.

Waking to the mystery of the Thing of things,
live in peace that passes the understanding of things.

EXISTED

...in memory of Agha Shahid Ali

Tell me what was I like before I existed—
was I dust or OM before my cry existed?

Do you remember the myriad hues of love
before the infinite blue of my sky existed?

The sky, beyond itself, was beside itself
when it discovered such a high existed.

Destined to die, my words forgotten, chances of
falling asleep to a lullaby existed.

Bereft of hope, I meditate like a butterfly,
thankful that a heaven of sighs existed.

How long must I wait for the darkness to lift,
believing that an impartial eye existed?

I have forgiven the universe and its Maker—
why tell the world a beautiful lie existed?

The waiting is over, time to leave, kiss farewell—
a joy to learn such loving goodbyes existed.

When I die, forgive and forget my failures,
speak not of what I was like before *I* existed.

TONIGHT

Is it love that prevents me from sleeping tonight—
the full moon's splendour or her silent weeping tonight?

Who sends these messages of love, what lies beneath
these tears of joy that will not stop leaping tonight?

None can see the dark side of the moon. Escape from
the darkness around you, see the light gift-wrapping the night.

What cannot be seen is imagined. Who is the archer
whose shafts tipped with truth are sweeping the night?

Much has been given in life, so much more withheld.
Tell me what's fair and what's unfairly creeping tonight?

My enemies have filled the skies with their slogans—
how can I stop their lies from entrapping the night?

Where are my friends, why are they silent—
is there a reward for betrayal, for gossiping tonight?

Fashions come and go, some things are forever—
what is not eternal is not for keeping tonight.

My treasures lie under a bed of forget-me-nots—
where else could I have hidden them for safekeeping tonight?

For how long must one *rage against the dying of the light*?
The stars have not stopped worshipping tonight.

I have not sought awards, titles, fame or riches—
what will I do with trinkets fools keep heaping tonight?

Who knows whose songs will be heard on people's lips?
What you have sown, my love, you can't stop reaping tonight.

WEATHERING

Forgotten in the backwater of time,
once entrusted to shine a light on darkness,

steering sailors and pilots away from danger,
from treacherous coasts to safe havens,

the lighthouse now stands abandoned, alone,
possessing a haunting beauty all its own.

Once home to gods, now a relic of the past,
the island offers sanctuary to seals, shelters

sea lions; lets earth's gorgeous creatures
breathe new life and purpose. Even the dead

sparkle for those who can see their splendour.
Those who can hear their songs, listen.

Wild, weird, wonderful—their music holds
us in thrall, dancing auroras.

Spinning in love's magnetic field, they light
up the sky with their incandescence.

Life and love are full of sighs, full of ecstasy.
Weathering is what we are here for—

to acquire that patina shine of self-realisation
before returning to the universe where we belong.

IN MEMORIAM

for my brother, Susanta Acharya,
who died of cancer aged 63
26 May 2024

I sought my soul, but my soul I could not see. I sought my God, but my God eluded me. I sought my brother and I found all three.
Unknown

A brother is a treasure, a gift from the universe to make life's journey a little less lonely.
Unknown

WE ARE ALL RETURNING

I

Grateful we'd been spared unimaginable loss
during a once-in-a-lifetime pandemic,

our family reunion was a blessing beyond words—
miraculous our gift, a thanksgiving like no other.

Then life delivered a googly. Alone at the crease,
bearing the weight of the world, you played your part.

A roll of the dice suddenly changed everything.
We were unprepared for such a cosmic glitch.

Unable to decipher the hieroglyphs of life—
it was love that held us together.

There is no way of knowing what we don't know.
Whether we know it or not, we are on a journey of our own.

Knowing the world is full of pain and suffering,
might it not be possible to dream we are born for happiness—

to love, be loved, and life immensely valuable?
The only way through this unknowing is Love—

amazement of the gods, miracle that resurrects
every moment of our lives—truth that sets us free.

The most revolutionary thing one can do in the worst
of times is to live and love to the best of one's ability.

So we loved and lived, more intensely than ever—
the extent of our love a measure of our humanity.

II

You never gave up hope, nor did we.
Braver than any warrior, you endured unbearable pain.

The hardest lesson for us was realising
our inability to take away your suffering.

Living with the injustices of the world, we held
on to courage and compassion as our precious
world began to fray at the margins.

Days disappeared without the light of your smile,
the music of your laughter, your wit and humour.

Watching each treatment annex your spirit,
your freedom, your passion for life ebbing like cinders

prepared us painfully for your departure.
Memories of your endless acts of love, our lifeline.

Seeing your life dissolve in losses, watching helplessly
the castle of your dreams falling off the edge of a precipice,
we held on to miracles as we began to lose everything.

III

There are times one is reduced to nothing—
lost the ability to live in uncertainty,
unable to make peace with ourselves or the world.

We have given it names, the unravelling of such forces—
bhagya, destiny, kismet, luck, language of the universe.

To dwell in mysteries deep as creation requires
the patience of ancient trees, holding on to life
in the bewildering metropolis of not-this-not-that.

Talking of things beyond human comprehension,
beyond our reckoning universes of blessings ruined by us.

God may work in ways unfathomable to humans—
it is humans who act in ways more unfathomable than gods.

The world may be illusion, nothing is more real than pain—
your pain the profoundest of prayers the gods would've heard.

None has found an answer to the existence of suffering.
Is faith something constant, not a candle flickering in the wind?

Were you blessed with faith, not struck with uncertainty,
faced with the nature and existence of God?

Doubting is one way of believing—
we doubt so we may walk in hope, live in possibility.

Thinking there must be something I could do to relieve your pain,
reaching out to the universal soul, I encounter silence,

a nothingness that shatters me. Is life a series of random outcomes?
And we humans here merely to add meaning?

If there's a force for truth and justice, enlighten me
so I may make sense of this unbearable darkness of being?

IV

During my daily conversations with the One
who bound our fates here on earth, ensured your presence

in my thoughts and prayers, I share my confusion.
We are the loneliest of beings in this world of unknowing.

Who can say why your journey home was so fraught,
why our world ended in losses we can never recover from?

Nothing in life is certain, regardless of what we do
or don't. There is no God to save us from
the complexities and limitations of being human.

How can one not believe in miracles, give Life
a chance as long as consciousness flows in us?

The world ends if we fail to protect lives entrusted to us.
When we can be the best of creation, why be the worst?

This the price of freedom—the strength to choose life and love.
Nothing can ever come to any good if we fail to fight

for what is universally, indisputably good.
And, goodness is life, love—all things true and beautiful.

Unwavering in purpose, you were the change you wanted
to see in the world. Born to protect others,

you never placed yourself first, never gave
us a hint of storms gathering in your horizon.

Love is what our heart knows, love sufficient unto love,
and human life, beyond precious, full of wonder.

V

Nothing in our world may be perfect—
without imperfection, we would not exist.

The world may also come to an end
because of our imperfections.

You stood up for what you believed to be true
and right with the perfect quietness of heart—

your humility, a state of being…
Let me know what God is, is not.

The only thing we are left with in life is love.
As long as I live, you live in my heart and mind—

every memory cleansed by your presence.
A star in my firmament, your light keeps shining.

No longer defined by the limitations of your body,
your ashes immersed in the Ganges, you are at home
in the universe. It is to Love we are all returning.

WHERE DID HE GO?

...after Jalāl ud-Dīn Muḥammad Rūmī

Where did our handsome and generous beloved go?
That majestic, graceful tree, where did he go?

A festival of light, he spread his sparkle among us.
Is he in peace and bliss where he is? Where did he go?

All day long our hearts tremble like leaves in a storm.
At night, in our restlessness we wonder, where did he go?

Refrains of songs he loved transport us to realms unknown—
hearts broken by his absence moan: Where did our beloved go?

Lost and bereft, we question all who knew this treasure—
this soul-stirring companion, where did he go?

That lovely face, uplifting like a smile, where did he go?
He's not here, to what unknown 'there' did he go?

Where did our compassionate, courageous friend go?
That versatile, brilliant brother, where did he go?

We listen to the peacocks crying through the night—
do they miss him as we do, sky-calling: Where did he go?

We gather in the garden, talk to the plants weeping in the rain—
that tall, heavenly scented flower of the gods, where did he go?

We go to the rooftop, confess to the stars and constellations:
we scattered his ashes in the Ganges. Where did he go?

Is he now part of the universe? Our tears overflow like rivers...
Thinking of that pearl in the vast ocean, where did he go?

We are all returning. If his soul is with God,
and he's left this realm of ours, where did he go?

DEAR LIFE

My words I minister to like my children,
offer them the freedom to be themselves—

warn them of risks from the moment they are born,
their very existence an act of rebellion.

Their bones breathe the mystery of the universe,
summoning all to love the way singing does.

I'm haunted by the enormity of their grief—
of the equal and opposite possibility of limitless joy

if we let love be our unfailing guide, follow
our inner compass, refusing to relinquish

our fate to self-serving, self-appointed gods.
Let life realise dreams that spell the light,

speak in the tongues of trees, meditate on stars,
the smallest that burn slowly for ever, seeking

to summon the soul of every wanderer.
Words hold the key to their own mystery—

offer shelter, a cradle of bliss where one can linger,
listening to music you've never heard before

like the dazzle of cheetahs, tigers in ecstatic pursuit,
the luminescence of light whirling in earthly delight.

Knowing all my words are what others make of them,
I teach them compassion, forgiveness, understanding.

My words are prayers to comfort a fatally injured bird,
tend to it with the every thingness of love until it stops breathing.

I have nothing else to offer, dear Life—
words are what I breathe and eat, the clothes I wear,

dreams that sing me to sleep, silence that greets me awake:
words are the only wealth I possess—my truth, my love.

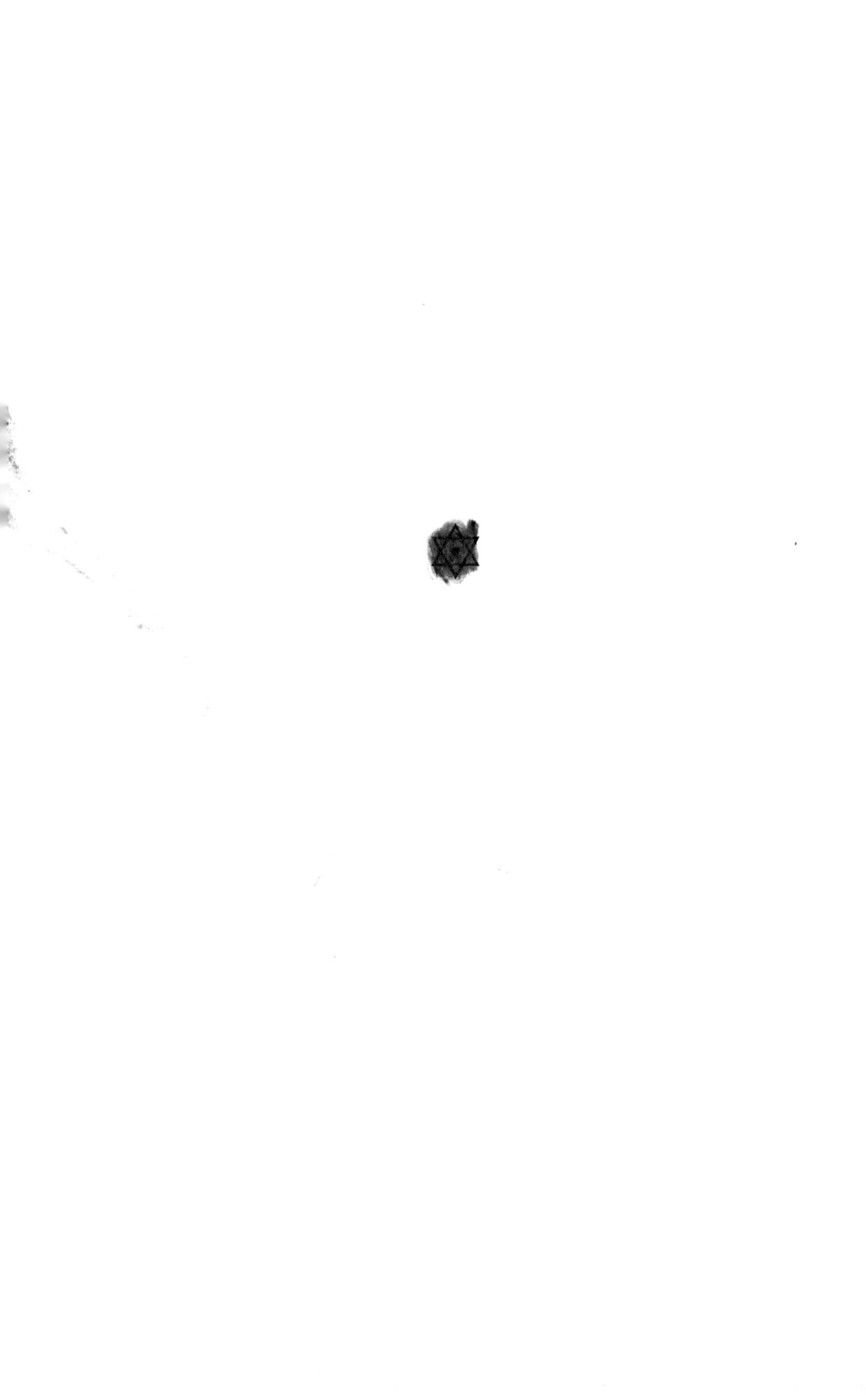

ACKNOWLEDGEMENTS

My thanks to the editors of the following publications in which several of these poems, or in earlier versions, first appeared:

Acumen, Agenda, A Glass of New Made Wine (1999), Amethyst Review, Atmos, At The Edge of All Storms (2022) (UK); The Beacon (India); Bengal Lights (Bangladesh); California Quarterly (US); Can You Hear The People Sing: Global Responses to the Pandemic (2020) (UK); The Challenge (India); Chiaroscuro Magazine (UK); Chipmunk (India); Confluence, Converse: Contemporary English Poetry by Indians (2022) (UK); Count Every Breath: A Climate Anthology (2023), Creative Flight (India); The Dance of the Peacock: An Anthology of English Poetry from India (Canada); The Dawntreader, Dreich (UK); Greening the Earth: A Global Anthology of Poetry (2023), Guftugu/Indian Cultural Forum (India); Gitanjali & Beyond (UK); I Can't Breathe: A Poetic Anthology of Social Justice (Kenya); Impressions, Indian Literature (India); The International Literary Quarterly (USA); The IUP Journal of Commonwealth Literature (India); Ink Sweat and Tears, The Interpreter's House (UK); Journal of Literature & Aesthetics (India); Journal of Postcolonial Writing (UK); Kavya Bharati (India); Life and Legends (USA); Das Literarisch (India); Live Encounters Magazine, Locked Down: Poems, diary extracts and art from the 2020 pandemic (2021), London Grip (UK); Madras Courier, Muse India (India); Musings During a Time of Pandemic: A World Anthology of Poems on COVID-19 (2020) (Kenya); Nth Position, Other Poetry, Pentacle Poetry, Plant Care: A Festschrift for Mimi Khalvati (2004), Poems on Conflict: Members of The Hall Writers' Forum (2022) (UK); The Punch Magazine, Quesadilla and Other Adventures: Food Poems (2019) (India); Radar Magazine (Russia); Rebel Talk: Poems from the Climate Emergency (2021) (UK); Re-Markings, Rhetorica (India); Scintilla: The Journal of the Vaughan Association, Sentinel Literary Quarterly (UK); Setu (USA); The Spectator, Spilling Cocoa Over Martin Amis, Stand Poetry Magazine (UK); Strands Lit Sphere (India); Tiger Moth Review (Singapore); Turning Pages: An Annual Creative Journal at Chemnitz University of Technology (Germany); Usawa Literary Review (India); Valparaiso Poetry Review (USA); Voices For The Silent (2022) (UK); Voices Now: World Poetry Today (2023) (India); Words for the Wild, Word Masala Award Winners 2015: An Anthology (UK); World Poetry Yearbook 2014 (China); Yearbook of Indian Poetry in English 2020-21 (India); Yearbook of Indian Poetry in English 2023 (UK).

My thanks and gratitude to Lance Lee for the gift of *Dear Life*. Special thanks to my brother, Sanjay Acharya, for the photographs. Without the support of family and friends, none of this would have been possible.

NOTES

Nesting: During the COVID pandemic, women and children suffered abuse greater than before in the UK. Previously, two women were killed by their partners every week.

Inside One's Own Singing: "The Soul selects her own Society" is the title line of the poem from Emily Dickinson. "When one has lived a long time alone" is the title line of the poem by Galway Kinnell.

Paradise In My Soul: 'The astonishing light of your own being!' is by Hafiz (My Brilliant Image). "Much Madness is divinest Sense'" is the title line of the poem by Emily Dickinson.

I Can't Breathe: On May 25th 2020, in Minneapolis, George Floyd was murdered by Derek Chauvin, a police officer, in broad daylight in the presence of witnesses who captured the tragic killing on video. While Chauvin was kneeling on Floyd's neck, three other officers stood by. Floyd repeatedly said he could not breathe, but the officers did nothing. The sad fact is the witnesses who captured the killing on video also failed to intervene. In the aftermath of this public execution, 'Black Lives Matter' protests erupted not only in America, but also in different parts of the world.

Afterwardsness: India became independent on 15 August 1947. The Partition of the Indian sub-continent by the British into Pakistan and India prior to Independence was conducted with indecent haste and lack of consideration for Hindus and Muslims who had lived together for almost four centuries. It generated such an atmosphere of hatred and revenge that the two communities turned against each other with unprecedented violence, resulting in large scale loss of life.

Looking For Myself: The title refers to a quote from Emily Dickinson, who wrote to a friend, "I am out with lanterns looking for myself," trying to describe how she felt moving into a new house. "Loneliness is a cramping/of the spirit for lack of companionship?" is a line by Doris Lessing in *The Grass Is Singing*.

The Questionnaire: *Air on the G String* refers to August Wilhelm's 1871 arrangement of the second movement of Johann Sebastian Bach's Orchestral Suite No 3 in D major.

Sunflower Seeds: "Putin treats Russian soldiers like logs thrown into a train's furnace," Ukrainian President Volodymyr Zelensky told *The Economist's* Zanny Minton Beddoes in a rare interview in Kyiv on 27 March 2022.

View From The Gods: The highest platform, or upper circle is known as the 'gods,' especially in large theatres, where the seats can be very high and a long distance from the stage. The quote *"unaccommodated man is no more but such a poor, bare, forked animal"* is from William Shakespeare (King Lear, Act 3, Scene 4).

The Reckoning: Poem inspired by *Christ Mocked (The Crowning with Thorns)*, a painting by Hieronymus Bosch in the National Gallery, London.

Be The Gods: "It takes a village to raise a child" is an African proverb.

Of Gods And Goddesses: Poem inspired by a visit to an open market in India where shop owners hang posters and calendars with alluring images of gods and goddesses resembling local film stars.

Hearing Eye: *"The most we can hope for/is that we might be understood by others/with different understandings/to ourselves."* is a quote from John Rety's penultimate poem in *What's in a Word?*, 1996.

Meeting *La Rêve* At The Tate Modern: Poem inspired by Picasso's painting seen at the Tate Modern exhibition in London, 'Picasso 1932—Love, Fame, Tragedy.'

The Tree Huggers: In 1730, Amrita Devi and her three daughters were slain along with 294 men and 68 women, belonging to the Bishnois community, while protecting a grove of Khejri trees (Prosopis Cineraria, sacred to the Bishnois) in Khejarli, Rajasthan. The Maharaja of Jodhpur's men had come to collect the wood of these trees to build a palace.

Tonight: The quote *"rage against the dying of the light"* is from "Do Not Go Gentle Into That Good Night" by Dylan Thomas, written in 1951.

GLOSSARY

Abhimanyu: In the ancient Hindu epic, *Mahabharata*, he is the son of Arjuna, a celebrated warrior. Abhimanyu's mother was the younger sister of Krishna. Raised by his maternal family, he was one of the few individuals, along with his father, who knew how to enter Chakravyuha, a powerful military formation. But, he did not know how to exit it. He was unfairly killed in the Kurukshetra War at the age of sixteen. He played a significant role in deciding the outcome of the war.

Arapaima: A very large freshwater fish capable of weighing 400 pounds and capable of reaching ten feet in length found in South America, notably in the Amazon.

Bhagya: In Sanskrit, it means fate, good luck, and destiny, among other traits.

Bishnois: A sect within Hinduism who believe in the sanctity of life. Eight of the twenty-nine commandments they follow relate to the conservation and protection of trees and animals. Their sacrifice, characterised by ahimsa (non-violence), led to a royal decree by the same Maharaja whose soldiers were responsible for their massacre in 1730, prohibiting the cutting of trees and causing harm to animals and birds in any Bishnoi village.

The Bishnois inspired the Chipko movement (chipko means 'to cling' in Hindi) that started in the 1970s, when a group of peasant women in the Himalayan hills threw their arms around trees designated to be cut down. They were also called the 'tree huggers.' This method of non-violent resistance, known as tree satyagraha, spread across India, forcing reforms in forestry and a moratorium on tree felling in the Himalayan region. It inspired other green activist movements across the world.

Brahma Kamala: This is a flowering plant native to the high mountain meadows of the Himalayas in Bhutan, India, Nepal, Pakistan and southwest China. Its image appears on the cover.

Broken Hill: Australia's oldest continuous mining area.

Bucha, et alia: Bucha is in the Ukraine, a Russian massacre site of Ukrainians: the others in this list are also massacre sites spread around the world.

Caravansarais: Buildings to provide overnight housing for travellers.

Chakravyuha: A powerful military formation.

Chanderis: Silk saris, originally derived from town of Chanderis.

Cuttack: The author's birthplace in India, in the province of Odisha, on the east coast of India.

Dasvidaniya: Goodbye, in Russian.

Dharma: In Hinduism, both a cosmic law of the right behaviour and social order, and the true nature of reality.

Durbar: The word is of Persian origin. It was first linked to ceremonial assemblies marking the proclamation of Queen Victoria as the Empress of India in 1877. It has since been referred to a court or public audience, some of a ceremonial nature, in India and other British colonies.

Durga: A goddess made by the gods to fight a demon, an enemy, only a woman could fight: a goddess of great, protective power.

Firangi: Not just foreigner, but outsider, alien. The Mughal dynasty in India applied it at first to every Christian.

Gaijin: Japanese for foreigner.

Ghar: Home, in Sanskrit.

Govinda: Name for Krishna and Vishnu, with meanings ranging from someone who pervades all worlds to Krishna disguised once as a loving cowherder.

Khejri: Trees (see Notes: The Tree Huggers, above).

Krishna: Krishna symbolizes love, patience, and tenderness. He is both an avatar of the great god in Hinduism, Vishnu, as well as a great god in his own right. Often he is thought of as humanity's protector.

Kurukshetra War: The war in the *Mahabharata* took place in the fields of Kurukshetra located in the state of Haryana in today's India.

Madrasa: An Islamic school.

Mahabharata: An ancient Hindu epic, it is about the struggle between two groups of cousins. For Hindus, it serves as a philosophical and spiritual text on every aspect of life and human behaviour.

Mandala: A sacred space. It can be a visual, geometric figure which represents the universe in Hinduism (and Buddhism). It can also be an image expressing a dream search for selfhood.

Mantra: A chant to help concentration, usually of a word or syllable, like "Om."

Muwashshah: Refers to an Arabic poetic form and a secular musical genre.

Namaste: A word of greeting in Hindu, literally meaning 'I bow to you.'

Naraka: The Sanskrit word for the Hindu Hell, and also a demon.

Panch puran: Five spices used in Indian cooking which includes equal measures of fenugreek, nigella, cumin, black mustard, and fennel.

Phulka: A roti flatbread.

Pomace: An olive oil that may reduce some cardiovascular diseases because it is highly refined, and doesn't contain polyphenols.

Propolis: A substance created by honeybees.

Pugli: In various Indian languages, refers to a female who is considered foolish, mad, lacking judgement, or is simply different. It is also a term of endearment.

Purdah: A Muslim and Hindu practice of separating women in a separate room or behind a curtain from men.

Radha: A favoured consort of Krishna, associated with success, wealth, and beauty; also an avatar of Lakshmi, the supreme goddess.

Ramayana: With the Mahabharata one of the two basic Indian Sanskrit epics.

Rasoi: Refers to cooking or the kitchen where it takes place in various north Indian languages.

Roti: A round flatbread native to the Indian subcontinent.

Shantih: Peace, and/or inner peace.

Salawāt: In Islam, refers to prayer.

Shamiana: Refers to outdoor coverings, awnings, or a ceremonial tent.

Shringara: Shringara has a rich association with the forms of love, as well as with an awareness of life's grand design, and a concern for living better, and more fully.

Sita: A Hindu goddess, and protagonist of the Ramayana. The wife of Rama, whose life is depicted in the Ramayana.

Souq: An open-air Arab market place.

Swayam: In Sanskrit means self, self-born, oneself.

Swayamvara: Refers to marriage in the Hindu traditions where a woman chooses the man she wishes as her husband, the 'vara' or the groom. The swayamvara is organized by the father of the bride. Vara has other meanings, such as 'wish.'

Vilayat: An Arabic word that was used during the Ottoman Empire to refer to a province or state. It was used to refer to the United States of America as well. In Urdu, the term Vilayat is used to refer to any foreign country. As an adjective, Vilayati is used to indicate an imported article or good. In Bengali and other Indian languages, the word is bilat and bilati, referring primarily to Britain and British-made. The British slang term 'blighty' derives from this word.

Vishwarupa darshan: Literally translates to a vision of the Divine, where the whole universe is contained within the universal form. Though there are multiple Vishwarupa theophanies, the most celebrated is in the *Bhagavad Gita*, part of the *Mahabharata*, where Krishna enlightens Arjuna on the battlefield of Kurukshetra.

Warramaba Virgo: A grasshopper species born from a single breeding 250,000 years ago and sexlessly remaining true to its kind pathogenetically with no ill effects.

AUTHOR'S BIOGRAPHICAL NOTE

Shanta Acharya is the author of twelve books, with *Dear Life* her eighth of poetry. *Imagine* drew together her selected poetry in 2017, followed by *What Survives Is The Singing* in 2020. Her poems have been translated into Bengali, Chinese, French, German, Hindustani, Odia, Russian, and Ukrainian.

Acharya was raised in Cuttack, India. One of the first women to be admitted to Worcester College in 1979, she was awarded a DPhil from Oxford. Her debut novel, *A World Elsewhere*, a powerful Bildungsroman, also explores a young Indian woman's journey to Oxford. A Visiting Scholar at Harvard in the department of English and American Literature and Languages, she returned to London and worked as an investment banker in the City. She continued to write poetry through all her upheavals and later founded and hosted the 'Poetry in the House' readings at Lauderdale House, Highgate, London, from 1996-2015. She served twice on the board of trustees of The Poetry Society as well as The Poetry School.

A free-lance writer and poet, she lives in Highgate, London. www.shanta-acharya.com